Tibbs the Meditation Cat

Mindfulness for Kids

10 9 8 7 6 5 4 3 2

First published in the United Kingdom by
North Star Press Ltd, 10 Harley Street, London W1G 9PF

A division of
North Star Group Ltd, 10 Harley Street, London W1G 9PF

A CIP catalogue record is available for this book from the British Library.

ISBN: 978-0-9553629-7-2
    1. Mindfulness 2. Success – Psychological Aspects

Printed and bound in the United States and the United Kingdom by Ingram Book Group Inc/Lightning Source Ltd
USA: 1246 Heil Quaker Blvd, La Vergne, TN 37086
UK: Chapter House, Pitfield, Kiln Farm, Milton Keynes MK11 3LW

The information in this book is given in good faith and belief in its accuracy at the time of publication, and may be subject to change. This book is not intended to provide personalised motivational, psychological or medical advice. Readers are encouraged to see the counsel of competent professionals when it comes to such matters as psychological and medical wellbeing.

The author and the publisher specifically disclaim, so far as the law allows, any and all liability, loss or risk, personal or otherwise, that is incurred as a consequence, either directly or indirectly, of the application and use of information contained in this book.

For consistency, British spelling, grammar and punctuation tends to be used throughout the book, as opposed to American conventions.

Development Editor: Max Eames
Illustrator: Philippa King (Instagram @philippa.king)
Deputy Art Editor: Angel Miguel Correa
Cover Designer: Shelley Bray
Layout Artist: SBCreative (info@sbcreative.org)

Foreword: A Note to Grown-Ups

Scientific evidence continues to suggest that mindfulness helps us improve our attention-spans, gain a greater sense of self-control, and develop a stronger sense of emotional resilience.

There is a strong sense that mindfulness might also contribute meaningfully to young people's wellbeing, resilience and character-development. Perhaps that's why the UK Government has commissioned an inquiry led by Members of Parliament. In addition to assisting with the acquisition of a number of skills and capabilities, it's considered that mindfulness might also serve to raise educational standards.

In response to the above enquiry, the Mindfulness All-Party Parliamentary Group (MAPPG) chose to outline a number of evidence-based recommendations in its October 2015 Government report. These are arguably *exciting* developments.

So, what exactly *is* it that has caused British parliamentarians to stand up and take notice? After all, mindfulness can be a big word – and a big concept – for many of us to take to heart.

With kids; especially younger kids; it's enough to say that mindfulness is about awareness. It's nothing more than noticing our present-moment feelings, our thoughts, and how our body feels.

When it comes to us grown-ups, for some reason the term 'mindfulness' seems to conjure up images of dedication, practice and deep soul-searching – but it's quite the opposite, actually. Mindfulness is an awareness we can each bring to bear in our own unique way. In fact, it's far from difficult to incorporate mindfulness into your life.

Even more exciting, pretty much *anybody* can learn its basic principles. It's not the least bit necessary to know one jot about the historical developments and the links to meditation – or to study the emerging body of research that seeks to explain the 'science' behind the timeless principles of mindful awareness.

If you're a complete novice when it comes to mindfulness, then you'll be relieved to know that it has nothing to do with intense concentration or focused effort.

Aside from cats, of course, it turns out that *children* are the best teachers of mindfulness principles – and we grown-ups have a lot to learn about re-orienting ourselves to the state of 'natural mindfulness' that is commonplace in a child's early years.

Maybe it helps to cast your mind back. *You* were a child once. Don't you remember being totally absorbed while flying a kite, making a sand castle or eating an ice-cream cone?

You used to *play* with your food, rather than eat it. And you did so without worrying about mussing up your shirt with gravy, eating your vegetables... or washing the dishes afterward. So, what *happened*?

Somewhere along the way, your ability to live in the present moment – without a care in the world – was quietly forgotten.

Our early years are those of enviable freedom in which to live life mindfully – so why on earth would we wait until kids have to *unlearn* a number of things in order to re-learn how to be mindful?

That sense of pure living – without the need to produce or perform – is the natural habitat of children. In fact, if you've decided that you'd like to teach your child the simple principles outlined in this book, you'll want to remember a timeless truth – kids often teach us a whole lot *more* than we do them.

Keep in mind, however, that kids typically learn best by example. The best way to teach mindfulness to kids is to practice it yourself. For either of you, it's best to start off with short timeframes – perhaps five minutes or less.

Some children – as well as adults – find the first attempts uncomfortable, and it's common to be a bit fidgety. Encouragement and praise will go a long way in the beginning – so short bursts might be best. It also helps to spend time afterward doing something you both enjoy, while you share your experiences.

With regular and short bursts of practice, you'll find that 'being mindful' amounts to a set of simple techniques that soon become second nature. Eventually, it's easy to go back to that 'place' of focus – and kids of all ages (I include myself in this category) can learn to do this entirely of their own accord, just like Tibbs!

Max Eames,
Development Editor

Acknowledgments

Firstly, I'd like to thank the three men in my life; Dan for all his support, Toby for his smiles and laughter, and Bernhard for sharing our love and joy.

I'd especially like to thank artist and illustrator Philippa King, for her beautiful illustrations, which were done with so much dexterity – and with the able assistance of her feline friend Jacky. Philippa has succeeded in bringing Tibbs's special personality and sense of fun to life, doing so with such generosity, patience and humour.

Next, much gratitude goes out to cover designer and layout artist Shelley Bray. Shelley brought a sense of playful fun to this project, and for that the entire team is indebted to her.

In turn, I'd like to thank deputy art editor Angel Miguel Correa. His inspiration and artistry lent the team a great deal of motivation at critical stages, and every page bears his imprint and sense of journalistic style.

Lastly, much appreciation extends to development editor Max Eames. We've remained special friends, and I'm happy our paths crossed so long ago, as if by the hand of fate.

Introduction

You're no doubt reading this now because, as a parent and/or a kid-at-heart, you've been witness to the young people around you participating in the 'always-on' and 'technology-enabled' world that is part and parcel of modern-day life. Perhaps you've become a little bit resigned to the implicit values associated with today's technology. Or maybe there are times when you remember your *own* childhood; arguably one of sharp contrast; with some degree of frustration and possibly concern.

How did life get so complicated? And what could – or should – be done about it, for the sake of the young people in your life? Especially when, in many ways, they've known of little else?

Within today's commonplace success-driven and efficiency-driven worldview, a whole lot of us – kids and adults alike – have occasionally forgotten how to give ourselves (and each other) the moments of attention we all crave and need. In our concerted effort to stay on top of things, it's easy to forget that things weren't always like they are in today's modern world.

The origins of mindfulness actually date back thousands of years, and are grounded in Hindu and Buddhist philosophies. Our present-day interest in mindfulness, infused with an inevitably *Western* context, was first brought to mainstream awareness in the 1960s.

In what we now refer to as the Swinging Sixties, a number of Westerners travelled to the East in order to discover and learn about meditation and yoga. Amongst these travellers were the likes of The Beatles, Leonard Cohen and a group of noted artists. Partly because of their notoriety, the public appeared keen to draw wisdom from various Eastern philosophies, and this newfound interest inspired a number of yogis and Zen teachers to travel to the West in order to share their insights.

For quite some time, however, accessibility would have been hampered by the fact that very little in written form was translated into English. This situation changed when the Vietnamese monk Thich Nhat Hanh; born in 1926; wrote *The Miracle of Mindfulness*, and permitted it to be translated with a great deal of care into English.

The first 'print run' of *The Miracle of Mindfulness* was a hundred copies, and since then it has been translated into several other languages. Thich Nhat Hanh has been a prolific author; at this stage he has penned over 100 more books. Many have thus encountered his wisdom through the written word, but others have been inspired through hearing him share his message of peace.

The first run of *The Miracle of Mindfulness* was brought to bear using a tiny offset printer, and assembled in an equally tiny bathroom. Stories such as this make most of us smile; after all, kids and adults alike are inundated with so much technology and technical devices that we take their relative ease-of-use for granted.

Our smartphones, tablets and computers mean that people of all ages can live an 'always-on-always-available' daily life. This has its pluses and minuses. The "Did you get my email? I sent it an hour ago" follow-up by text is a byword of the technological revolution we've witnessed and become part of.

What this means in practice is that a great many of us – kids and adults alike – don't seem to remember when or how to simply 'be'. The sneaky peek at the phone is commonplace at the kitchen table, in the cinema, while waiting for a bus, or even in the bathroom! One consequence of this constant accessibility and alertness to incoming information is; at least for some; a near-total lack of peace.

Mindfulness thus stands to offer many of us a sense of greater awareness within this complex world in which we live. It also offers us a chance to view such complexity from a slightly different perspective, if only for a few moments a day. It's in essence an invitation you can give yourself – one of reconnecting to moments of simplicity in life. All that is required, really, is a slight and momentary shift in your focus and awareness.

Such momentary shifts can allow you to get to know yourself a shade better. These mini-breaks can remind you of your own ways in which to remain in contact with the parts of yourself that you tend to set aside when living the 'always-on' mindset of modern-day living. Your feelings, your bodily sensations, and your idle thoughts can all be welcomed openly and with fuller awareness.

Although mindfulness can help you to reconnect, at the *same* time it maintains just enough distance for you to observe yourself with wisdom, curiosity and self-compassion. In fact, allowing our experiences to 'simply be' often provides us a gateway through which we can learn more about the 'whys' and the 'hows' of what we think, do and feel.

Once we understand our own selves a bit better, we stand to gain better insight into the thoughts, actions and feelings of those around us. Broadly speaking, this holds true for people of all ages and stages of development. In that sense, the value of mindfulness – in terms of our relationship with those we love and care for – cannot be underestimated.

Whether you are six years old or sixty, there is a wisdom in seeing your life and its unrealised potential as a gift. Keep in mind, however, that mindfulness is about experiencing what life is offering at a given point in time. It means accepting instances of boredom, frustration and unease; being with those moments as fully as you possibly can.

One thing I remind myself during such times is that every moment of our lives represents the frontier of an entirely new beginning. It's as true for you as it is for me; each passing moment is full of potential, and each moment is an opportunity for change or acceptance.

Whatever your age; whatever your present circumstances: enjoy one of life's truths; namely, that it is only when we look beyond life's limitations that we can glimpse our true selves. And it is only in this 'now' that we can make a difference, and experience life to the fullest. In that sense, mindfulness is much more than a sense of awareness. It's a lifestyle open to each and every one of us; one of openness, adventure, patience and a healthy dose of childlike curiosity. So, why not live in the moment, starting right now?

With blessings,
Patrizia Collard, PhD

Tibbs the Meditation Cat

My cat is called Tibbs, which is short for Tybalt. His is an ancient name used by the famous playwright William Shakespeare.

If you know the story of *Romeo and Juliet*, you might also know that Tybalt (known as the 'king of cats') was Romeo's rival.

1

Tibbs loves roaming about outside – usually in the middle of the night. He is *just* like his Shakespearian namesake... who was also referred to as the Prince of the Night.

Did you know that, long before Shakespeare's time, cats used to be thought of as gods and goddesses in ancient Egypt?

They certainly appear regal and full of presence, don't they?

Yes, Tybalt is certainly a special cat… and this is why he was given his *very* special name.

Like *most* cats, however, Tibbs doesn't like a fuss made over him. He is usually quite happy on his own, looking for adventure with other cats in the neighbourhood.

With people, however, he tends to be happiest when they are together in a nice, warm room… sitting in stillness.

Tibbs always seems to feel relaxed and safe, as he connects with the people in the room. Sometimes he joins them in what is known as *meditation.*

You might be wondering what *meditation* actually is.

I think you would understand meditation by
imagining that you were totally 'at one' with
a favourite thing... something you *especially*
love doing.

For example, suppose right now you were licking an ice cream… and *really* tasting its flavours, enjoying its coolness as you felt it on your tongue.

As you were enjoying your ice cream, you might be noticing (sometimes with a little sadness) how, with each lick, the ice cream itself becomes less and less... until finally it is gone.

Even so, each lick would be an experience of great delight. What's *your* favourite kind of ice cream? Maybe you'd like to imagine it now.

All the while, you might still have the taste in your mouth… and possibly on your fingers or around your mouth.

Hopefully not on your favourite T-shirt!

With or without ice cream, *meditation* connects you deeply with your senses... as well as the world around you.

Meditation helps you to be 'deeply connected' with your favourite things.

Tibbs, for example, spends *loads* of time each day... just on grooming and mindfully licking his furry coat.

He sometimes also does a bit of scratching...
the whole time generally making himself (and
particularly his tail) look shiny and beautiful.

He ends up sparkling like the night sky when he
is done.

Most of the time, Tibbs is entirely devoted to... well... just being *comfortable*. Cats are such lucky creatures, aren't they?

In a way, for us people, cats are also excellent teachers.

That's because cats help us remember to sometimes *enjoy* things as they are... instead of constantly doing, doing, doing – and trying to be so *busy* all the time.

Tibbs chooses to hang out with us when we are being mindful: just sitting, lying down or standing... even when we are doing *nothing* in particular.

Actually, perhaps I should say... at least we *seem* to be doing nothing in particular.

When we meditate,
sometimes we watch a
single object for a long
while… and it looks
as if we are in a daze or
almost asleep.

At other times, we simply focus on little more than
feeling how our breath enters, and then leaves,
our body.

It feels as if the breath expands our chest and belly like a *balloon* on the in-breath… and on the out-breath, the same parts of our body *deflate* – just like when you let go of a balloon without tying up the end.

During meditation, we can also take an imaginary journey through our body... visiting each and every body-part, occasionally letting go – on the out-breath – of any uncomfortable tension we might notice along the way.

This is a fun exercise known as the Body Scan.

Sometimes we meditate by simply listening to the sounds around us, as they seem to come and go.

Tibbs certainly enjoys doing all of these practices with us... and a whole lot more, as well.

Tibbs also likes to sit on our bellies, lie between our legs, curl up in front of us, or stretch… just like *we* do when we practice what is known as 'mindful' movement.

Usually Tibbs lies right in the middle – maybe pretending to be the object we are all focused on when we meditate.

At other times he props himself on top of a radiator, a chest of drawers or the nearest chair.

Then again, he often
lies right *in between* two
people… as if he were
ready to join in
with them.

Tibbs *certainly* likes being the centre of attention. When he 'adopts' you, you can just decide to accept it… and *wait* until he grows tired of you.

And why *not* – he really is lovely!

Tibbs also shows his affection by brushing up against people's legs – *especially* when they are sat at the table eating, mind you!

He is the sort of cat who hopes to be invited for a little taster of some of the 'people food'... and he *especially* loves cream and cheese. What about you? What are *your* most favourite foods?

After a nice meal, Tibbs likes to stroll around with us in the park that is just behind our house.

This is a magical place to walk mindfully, enjoy the smell of the grass, take in the view of the flowers and trees... and of course watch the 'movie' of the clouds as they float across the sky.

Tibbs often sits on the trees we are leaning on… or sometimes hugging. Have you ever seen anyone hug a *tree* in a park? It looks *very* funny, but it's also fun to do.

Especially after we have been meditating, Tibbs likes us to stroke him gently... which he simply adores.

But even if nobody is around meditating, Tibbs likes doing his *own* stretches and cat-style meditations.

Tibbs never needs to be shown how to have a fabulous time. It all seems to come about so *naturally* to him.

Tibbs is totally at ease when he meditates, and we all love him for being so 'mindful' around us.

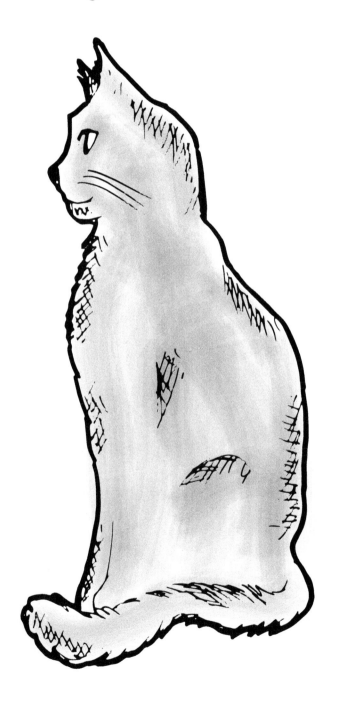

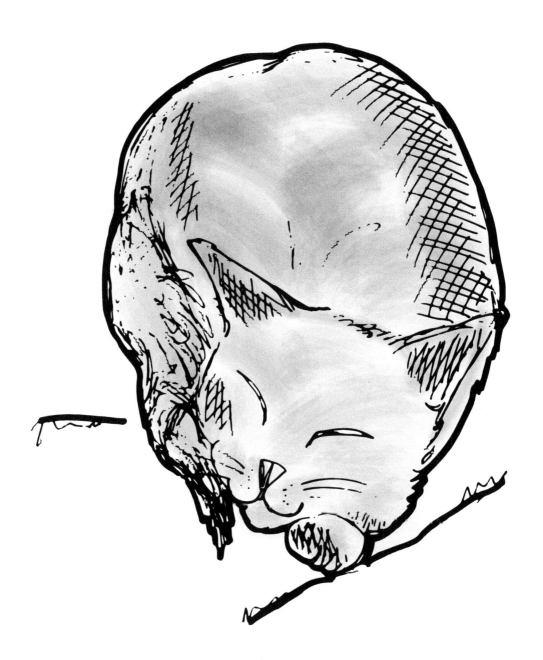

Time spent with this lovely creature is certainly time that's never wasted… and somehow Tibbs seems to have *all* the time in the world!

But you might *still* be wondering why people – and cats such as Tibbs – choose to *meditate*.

Do you remember moments when you simply *listened*, and maybe did nothing else?

Perhaps you can remember listening to the rain pattering on the roof of your bedroom at night... or the waves of the sea swishing endlessly back and forth... back and forth?

Or maybe a time when you've watched the birds flying in the sky...

or the branches of some trees 'waving' to each other in a strong wind?

Some people just like being stretched out on the floor... and that's enough to make them feel relaxed, calm and happy.

For me, all of these relaxing activities are what *meditation* is all about.

Meditation can be *anything* we like to do – any activity that helps us sense peace and joy, in the very simple... but special... moments of our lives.

Guess what? While I am sat at my desk writing this little book, Tibbs is resting on a tall chest of drawers… calmly watching me, and looking *very* relaxed indeed.

I suppose this means that Tibbs the 'meditation cat' has *enjoyed* our little story. And I certainly hope *you* have, too!

THE END

About the Author

Patrizia Collard, PhD is a mindfulness teacher, psychotherapist, stress management consultant and lecturer in psychotherapy at the University of East London. Her books include *Journey into Mindfulness, Mindfulness-Based Cognitive Therapy for Dummies, The Little Book of Mindfulness, The Mindfulness Bible,* and *Awakening the Compassionate Mind.*

Lightning Source UK Ltd.
Milton Keynes UK
UKOW07f1214111216
289239UK00030B/51/P